B-17 F Fortress
Nose Art Gallery

John M. and Donna Campbell

Motorbooks International
Publishers & Wholesalers ®

First published in 1993 by Motorbooks International Publishers & Wholesalers, PO Box 2, 729 Prospect Avenue, Osceola, WI 54020 USA

Library of Congress Cataloging-in-Publication Data
Campbell, John M.
      B-17 Flying Fortress nose art gallery/John M. Campbell, Donna Campbell.
         p. cm.
      Includes index.
      ISBN 0-87938-747-5
      1. B-17 bomber—History. 2. Airplanes, Military—United States—Decoration—History. 3. World War, 1939-1945—Aerial operations, Am. 4. Korean War, 1959-1953—Aerial operations, American. I. Campbell, Donna II. Title.
UG1242.B6C36   1993
358.4'283'0973—dc20   93-1161

Printed and bound in Hong Kong

On the front cover: The beautifully restored B-17G *Miss Museum of Flying*. Michael O'Leary

On the back cover: Top left, the B-17F *Miss Barbara*. Top right, the B-17F *Miami Clipper*. Lower right, the B-17F *Shawano*. Lower left, the B-17G *Tiger Girl*.

Contents

Acknowledgments

We would like to thank the many people who took time to give us advice, assistance, and encouragement: Gary James, Mike Conners, Charles Rukes, Wayne Watts, Jeff Ethel, Jamie Romey, Jamie Jones, Eulene Harber, Judy Willoughby, Betty Duval, Betty Bounds, John Farmer, Stan Alexander, Don Alexander, E.J. Hunter, Bob Young, Virgil Frazier, Terry Davis, Gerald James, Tom Suminski, Cecil Logan, Gary Stout, John Wages, Jackie Williams, Kenny Webb, Charlie Kennedy, Mike Jaggers, Sharon Ray, Mike Green, Nick Veronico, Ed Kueppers, Mark Copeland, Mark Bacon, Wayne Walrond, Steve Pace, Fred Huston CAF, Maurice Belding, Gene White, Gene Burtwell, Robin Hubbard, Richard Grayson, Jay Reid, Ernie Cagle, Chuck Burton, Hardy Horton, Susan Davis, Garry Pape, (Mad) Mike Hill, Wes Henry, Theresa Privette, Jack McKee, Jerry McKee, Lisa McKee, Robert Snodgrass, Herman Hetzel, Ron Fish, Pat Williams, Steve Wilson, Darryl Moore, Douglas Legg, Kathy and Richard Long, Kevin Grantham, Claude Cranfield, and most especially to Jess and Jewell Easton, David and Jesslyn Parrin, Joshua and Regina Feemster, Jim and Ann Ingram, Julie Long, and Robert and Christy Miller. I want to thank my mother and father, Ruth and F. D. Campbell, for everything they have done to help me along in my interest and research.

Bless them all....

Introduction

The B-17 is spoken of with affection by the crewmen who served in her. "Beautiful," "majestic," and "a powerhouse" are a few of the words used to describe the Flying Fortress, and she was all of these things and many more. The B-17 carried thousands of American flight crewmen into battle. She took to the air over and over to bomb Germany's heartland. The crews, faced with day after lengthy day, decided to decorate their ships with colorful slogans and paintings that expressed their feelings for things dear, as well as their opinions of things not so dear.

These paintings may have depicted the pilot's wife or sweetheart, or an image of Hitler getting his due. The art may have been inspired by a popular song or by a feeling of pride in the crew's home state or country. No matter what the feeling or the reason, the artists never seemed to run short of talent, ideas, or paint. The art itself was as varied as the men who dreamed up the colorful metaphors, the racy dames, femme fatales, and outrageous animals and creatures. All gave their essence to this form of expression.

We hope you enjoy this collection of art that reflects back to a unique time in our nation's history. Relax, enjoy, and let your imagination wander.

Nose Art Gallery

This photo of the B-17 *Mischief-Maker II*, serial 42-30412, was taken 8 November 1943. This aircraft served with the 339th Bomb Squadron, 96th Bomb Group.

This rendition of the grim reaper was on a B-17G named *Uninvited*. Note the bomb held by the skeleton hand.

Holy Mackeral! was a B-17F, serial 41-24609, that served with the 359th Bomb Squadron, 303rd Bomb Group.

This B-17F, serial 42-110157, served with the 491st Bomb Group and the 466th Bomb Group.

Stinky Weather was a B-17G, serial 42-31179, that served as a weather bird. Note that the mission markers are weather vanes.

The B-17F *Windy City Challenger* belonged to the 422nd Bomb Squadron, 305th Bomb Group.

The crew of the B-17G *Dear Mom* poses for a group photo to send home.

This bomb-tossing sky gremlin appeared on the B-17F, serial 42-30595, named *Gremlin Gus II*. This aircraft fought with the 560th Bomb Squadron, 388th Bomb Group.

The B-17G *Our Baby*, serial 42-31170, also flew for the weather service. Note the weather vanes marking its missions.

Stars and Stripes 2nd Edition was a B-17G from the 385th Bomb Group.

Stumble Butt was another of the weather-recon B-17s. This one was a G model carrying the serial 42-39777.

The B-17F *Tet Tittlite* is adorned with a painting of the regal American eagle, which is doing its best in the war against tyranny by dropping bombs on the enemy below.

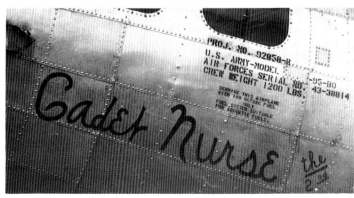

Cadet Nurse the 2nd, a B-17G, serial 43-38814, that served with the 336th Bomb Squadron, 95th Bomb Group, 8th Air Force.

This restored B-17G, *Aluminum Overcast,* had its photo taken at an air show at Tinker AFB, Oklahoma.

One of several versions of the bell as a belle in the art of World War II.

The post in this art lists the seven home states of the crew members. This B-17G, called *Hikin' for Home,* serial 42-107027, flew for the 322nd Bomb Squadron, 91st Bomb Group.

Although the name on this aircraft is hard to decipher, the weather-vane mission marks place it among those B-17s used for weather recon.

Maiden America takes on a new meaning on this B-17G. The box is labeled "High Explosives Tokio via Berlin Made in America."

The B-17F *Heinie Headhunters.*

The mission marks on this B-17G, *Leading Lady,* show a very successful career. Her crew poses with her on a rain-soaked runway.

Merry Ann was a natural-metal B-17G that served with the 91st Bomb Group. Tony Starcer painted the art.

The B-17F *Oklahoma Okie*, serial 42-29921, belonged to the 324th Bomb Squadron, 91st Bomb Group.

Miami Clipper, a B-17F, serial 42-29815, was assigned to the 322nd Bomb Squadron, 91st Bomb Group. This aircraft returned to the United States as a training ship at Amarillo Army Air Field.

Hitler's Gremlin pictures Hitler goose-stepping over an arrow. This art was on a B-17F that served with the 401st Bomb Squadron, 91st Bomb Group.

The 91st Bomb Group's B-17G named *Lady Helen of Wimpole* is being christened by Lady Helen.

This lovely young Indian maiden was on the B-17G *Redwing*, serial 43-38088, that served with the 322nd Bomb Squadron, 91st Bomb Group.

This camouflaged B-17G was named *Hairless Joe* after the comic book character. It may have fought with the 91st Bomb Group.

My Baby was a 91st Bomb Group B-17G.

The B-17F *Rebel's Revenge,* serial 42-29750, was assigned to the 323rd Bomb Squadron, 91st Bomb Group.

Idaliza was a B-17F, serial 42-97546, that served with the 360th Bomb Squadron, 303rd Bomb Group.

Bride of Mars is another of the 91st Bomb Group paintings by Tony Starcer. This is on a B-17G, serial 43-38360, that served with the 322nd Bomb Squadron.

This combination bee and B-17 was found on *She's A Honey,* a B-17G, serial 43-38961, that flew with the 305th Bomb Group.

This B-17F, *Delta Rebel No 2,* is preparing for takeoff. It fought with the 323rd Bomb Squadron, 91st Bomb Group and carried the serial 42-5077. Clark Gable was a crewmember on this aircraft.

Frenesi was a B-17G, serial 42-39775, that flew with the 333rd Bomb Squadron, 94th Bomb Group.

This graceful dove is seen on the B-17G *The Peacemaker,* serial 43-37552. This aircraft fought with the 401st Bomb Squadron, 91st Bomb Group.

Mister Yank-II was a B-17F, serial 42-5954, that served with the 562nd Bomb Squadron, 388th Bomb Group. Note the message on the bomb.

This B-17F, serial 42-30289, named *The Dull Tool*, fought with the 568th Bomb Squadron, 390th Bomb Group.

This 8th Air Force B-17F is named *Cincinnati Queen*. Its scoreboard shows that this picture was taken shortly after it entered the war.

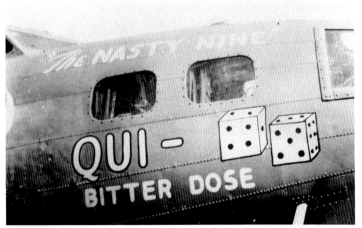

The Nasty Nine/ Qui-9 Bitter Dose, a B-17, serial 42-5468, belonged to the 360th Bomb Squadron, 303rd Bomb Group.

The Lucky Strike was a B-17F.

El-Diablo was the name of this B-17F, serial 42-3349, that served with the 332nd Bomb Squadron, 94th Bomb Group.

The JubJub Bird was a B-17G, serial 42-31883, that served with the 401st Bomb Squadron, 91st Bomb Group. The name came from the sound the aircraft made during warm-up.

The B-17G Nine O Nine carried the serial 42-31909, which is where it got its name. It was assigned to the 323rd Bomb Squadron, 91st Bomb Group.

The B-17G Miss Windy City.

An angry Uncle Sam is on the nose of this B-17F, *Yankee Doodle.*

The B-17F *Miss Fury* served in the Mediterranean Theater of Operations.

The Zoot Suiters, a B-17F, serial 42-30235, flew with the 412th Bomb Squadron, 95th Bomb Group.

These crew members stand by the nose of their natural-metal B-17G, *The Columbus Miss.*

Scarlett O'Hara was a B-17F from the 379th Bomb Group.

Sherry's Cherries was a B-17G, serial 42-97984, that served with the 401st Bomb Squadron, 91st Bomb Group.

The Vulture sports a vulture biting through the tail fuselage of an enemy aircraft.

Detroit Special was a B-17G used as a weather-recon aircraft.

This photo was taken as the name was applied to the B-17F *Slightly Dangerous*.

My Prayer was on a B-17F, serial 42-5712, that served with the 322nd Bomb Squadron, 91st Bomb Group.

Mercy's Madhouse, a B-17G, serial 42-97557, served with three different groups: the 303rd Bomb Group, the 305th Bomb Group, and the 384th Bomb Group.

The crew poses with its pride, the B-17G *Daddy's Delight*. This 303rd Bomb Group aircraft carried the serial 42-97944 and served with the 359th Bomb Squadron.

This B-17G, *Tower of London*, serial 44-8471, flew with both the 91st Bomb Group and the 369th Bomb Squadron, 306th Bomb Group.

This little guy, known as *Strato-Sam,* was seen on more than one B-17. This time he is saying, "Toughest Crew That Ever Flew...That's US!"

Demo Darling, serial 42-39774, fought with the 323rd Bomb Squadron, 91st Bomb Group.

This B-17G, serial 43-38202, was named *Miss Slipstream.* It fought with the 322nd Bomb Squadron, 91st Bomb Group.

The B-17F *Lightning Strikes,* serial 42-3073, flew with three different groups during its service: the 91st Bomb Group, the 94th Bomb Group, and the 388th Bomb Group.

The artist responsible for the great shark-mouth design on this B-17G, *Tiger Girl,* incorporated the chin turret into the design.

The B-17G *Anxious Angel* flew with the 91st Bomb Group.

Flaming letters form the name *Satan's Lady* on this B-17G.

Schnozzle, a B-17G, serial 42-40011, was named for the famous comedian Jimmy Durante and his outstanding profile. This B-17 fought with the 534th Bomb Squadron, 381st Bomb Group.

Boops, a B-17G, serial 44-83259, is preparing for takeoff. Note the metal covering where the chin turret is installed on most G models.

Lady Luck, sports a woman sitting on a bomb as though it were a bar stool.

Swamp Fire, a B-17G, serial 42-32024, that served with the 524th Bomb Squadron, 379th Bomb Group, shown after it completed 100 missions.

This B-17F, serial 42-5132, named *Royal Flush!,* has a winning hand up front. It flew with the 401st Bomb Squadron, 91st Bomb Group. Note the angry shark mouth on the antenna pod.

The stick character looks quite natural on this B-17G, *The Saint.*

The crew members of *The Princess Pat* take time to have their photo taken with their aircraft. This B-17F, serial 42-30829, was assigned to the 563rd Bomb Squadron, 388th Bomb Group.

Tempest Turner, a B-17G, serial 43-38216, served with both the 34th and 493rd Bomb Groups.

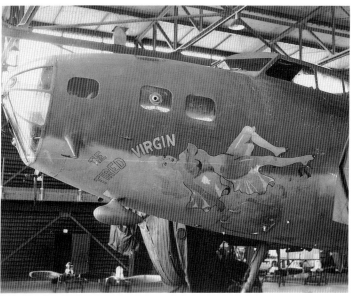

This B-17E, named *The Tired Virgin,* was used as a training fortress at the Amarillo Army Airfield during 1944 and 1945.

The B-17G named *I-Dood-It* sits stripped of her engines and guns at the Kingman, Arizona, boneyard after the war.

This fancy dresser was on *Duke of Paducah,* a B-17G, serial 42-37736, that served with the 324th Bomb Squadron.

The B-17G *Yankee Doodle Dandy.* Note James Cagney sitting with the guys just prior to christening the aircraft with the bottle of bubbly cradled in his arm.

Never Satisfied, a B-17F, is racking up an impressive scoreboard. Note the seven swastikas over the bomb missions.

This 11th Bomb Group B-17F, *Black Jack,* does it the easy way with an Ace and a Jack. It served in the Southwest Pacific.

The crew of this B-17F, *Flak Hack,* used the eight ball as its symbol. The serial of this aircraft, which served with the 360th Bomb Squadron, 303rd Bomb Group, was 42-97329.

This is one of several B-17s named *Piccadilly Commando*. This E model fought with the 322nd Bomb Squadron, 91st Bomb Group and carried the serial 42-3057.

As the scoreboard shows, this B17F, *Milk Wagon,* has been on many milk runs. Note the milk bottle mission marks.

This natural-metal B-17G was named *Blonde Bomber.*

This B-17, serial 42-29494, was called *Our Nel* and sported this dark-haired young lady on its vertical.

The B-17F *Hag of Harderwyk* shows a woman holding up the victory sign. Note the shell damage on the breast of the Hag.

Weary Bones, a B-17G, serial 42-37943, fought with the 368th Bomb Squadron, 306th Bomb Group.

Clark Gable stands with a group of crew members in front of *Delta Rebel No 2,* a B-17F, serial 42-5077, that served with the 323rd Bomb Squadron, 91st Bomb Group.

Surrounding the painting of Donald Duck are flak bursts on *Flak Happy,* serial 42-30367. This aircraft fought with the 337th Bomb Squadron, 96th Bomb Group.

The artist is finishing his work on a female version of Satan on this B-17. Just in front is a painting of the bombardier in his usual position.

Coy De Coy II, serial 42-30639, flew with the 569th Bomb Squadron, 390th Bomb Group.

Special Delivery, a B-17G, serial 42-102496, that fought with the 359th Bomb Squadron, 303rd Bomb Group.

Here we catch the artist Tony Starcer at work. *General Ike* was the work of both Starcer and White. It was on a B-17G, serial 42-97061, that served with the 323rd Bomb Squadron, 91st Bomb Group.

The 390th Bomb Group had its share of wild children; it had two B-17s named *Wild Children,* one *Wild Children II,* and one *Wild Children III.*

This B-17G, serial 44-6883, fought with the 535th Bomb Squadron, 381st Bomb Group. Note the insignia, which reflects the shared battle efforts of British and US forces.

The name *Jeannie* was on this natural-metal B-17G, number 034.

Virgin on the Verge was a B-17F, serial 42-5900, that served with the 561st Bomb Squadron, 388th Bomb Group.

The B-17F *Virgin Sturgeon.*

This B-17G, serial 44-6939, *Mizpah,* carried the prayer, "May the Lord watch over me and thee, while we are absent one from the other."

This is another *Virgin Sturgeon,* possibly the opposite side of the aircraft in the preceding photo.

Another *Mizpah.* This one has a crucifix just over the name.

The crew members of this B-17 pose by their favorite piece of art.

This aerial view shows the art on the B-17G *Piccadilly Lilly* a popular name for World War II aircraft.

I Got Spurs was a B-17F.

The B-17G *Hoosier Hot Shot.*

This star-spangled dancing lady was on a nameless B-17F.

The B-17G *Stage Door Canteen* is being christened in this photo. This aircraft, serial 42-31990, flew for the 535th Bomb Squadron, 381st Bomb Group.

The name *Phyllis* was found on several B-17s. This one was on the B-17G, serial 42-31067, that served with the 535th Bomb Squadron, 381st Bomb Group.

Vonnie Gal, a B-17G, serial 42-3524, fought with the 526th Bomb Squadron, 379th Bomb Group.

The *Jeannie Bee* was a natural-metal B-17G that served with the 570th Bomb Squadron, 390th Bomb Group. It carried the serial 43-37555.

Superman was on this B-17F, serial 41-24444, that served with the 340th Bomb Squadron, 97th Bomb Group.

The B-17F *Big Dick* had art on the nose and also the entry hatch.

The B-17G *Calamity Jane*.

The B-17F *Yankee Doodle Dandy*, serial 42-5264, flew for the 358th Bomb Squadron, 303rd Bomb Group.

This B-17F simply carried the name *Yankee Doodle*, but its scoreboard is quite impressive.

The crew is blessed before takeoff in this picture of the B-17G *Perpetual Help*, serial 43-38887. The aircraft, fought with the 751st Bomb Squadron, 457th Bomb Group. It also carried the name *Perpetual Hell*.

This B-17F is rare in that it carries a Russian name.

These crewmen of the 570th Bomb Squadron, 390th Bomb Group, pose in front of their B-17G, serial 42-312275, named *G.I. Wonder.*

Pregnant Portia, a B-17F, serial 42-30263, fought with the 551st Bomb Squadron, 385th Bomb Group.

Pist'l Packin' Mama, a B-17G, serial 42-37779, fought with the 324th Bomb Squadron, 91st Bomb Group.

Belle of the Blue, a B-17G, serial 42-102503, fought with the 423rd Bomb Squadron, 306th Bomb Group.

Fitch's Bandwagon, a B-17F, serial 42-107043, fought with the 613th Bomb Squadron, 401st Bomb Group. Note the majorette on the nose of the plane.

Dry Martini & The Cocktail Kids the 4th, a B-17F, fought with the 305th Bomb Group. Note the two ducks denoting decoy missions.

Lady Luck is clothed in a couple of eight balls, a scarf decorated with four-leaf clovers, and a horseshoe. She was on the B-17G, serial 42-012416, that served with the 349th Bomb Squadron, 100th Bomb Group.

Shangri-La Lil was a B-17F that served with the 360th Bomb Squadron, 303rd Bomb Group.

The B-17F *Hell's Angel*.

The B-17G *Petrol Packing Mama*.

The name *Thundermug* was used on several B-17s. This one is an F model that served with the 8th Air Force.

'Erberts Buddy was a B-17 that served with the 8th Air Force.

Accompanying the skull and crossbones on the tail of this B-17 is the name *Rat Poison*. Note the kill mark.

The B-17F *Phyllis*.

Double Trouble was a B-17F, serial 42-3082, that served with the 94th Bomb Group.

B-17F *Black Diamond Express,* serial 41-24416, served with the
359th Bomb Squadron, 303rd Bomb Group. In addition to its
art, it got zapped with names and home states.

This is the tail section of *Black Diamond Express,* showing more
names.

Miss Bea Haven, a B-17F, serial 42-5257, that served with the 359th Bomb Squadron, 303rd Bomb Group, after it was autographed by members of the group.

Yankee Doodle Dandy, a B-17F, serial 42-264, that served with the 358th Bomb Squadron, 303rd Bomb Group, also received the works as the group members said good-bye.

The tail section of *Miss Bea Haven.*

Another B-17F that served with the Hell's Angels, 303rd Bomb Group.

Wicked Witch fought with the 323rd Bomb Squadron, 91st Bomb Group.

Belle of the Blue, a B-17F, serial 42-30094, that fought with the 358th Bomb group.

The B-17F *Nemesis of Aeroembolism.*

Miss Shakmate, a B-17F that served with the 96th Bomb Group.

Blooming Grove, was a B-17F that fought with the 407th Bomb Squadron, 92nd Bomb Group.

Fools Rush In, was a B-17G, serial 42-31066, that fought with the 100th Bomb Group.

Fickle Finger of ? was a B-17F, serial 42335, that fought with the 385th Bomb Group.

Tondelayo was a B-17F, serial 42-29896, that served with the 379th Bomb Group.

Blue Dreams was a B-17G, serial 42-37761, that served with the 91st Bomb Group.

Liberty Belle was a 385th Bomb Group B-17F, serial 42-30096.

A 385th Bomb Group B-17G, *Blue Champagne.*

Roger Dodg'-Her, a B-17F, serial 42-30425, flew with the 333rd Bomb Squadron, 94th Bomb Group.

Shackeroo! II, a B-17, serial 42-29708, fought with the 332nd Bomb Squadron, 94th Bomb Group.

Dragon Lady was a B-17F, serial 42-30836, that fought with the 551st Bomb Squadron, 385th Bomb Group.

Tiger Girl was a B-17G, serial 42-3555, that fought with the 388th Bomb Group.

Latest Rumor was a B-17G, serial 42-3547, that fought with the 385th Bomb Group.

Snoozin' Susan was a 351st Bomb Group B-17F, serial 42-29860.

Bam Bam was a B-17G, serial 42-37893, that fought with the 303rd Bomb Group.

Ack-Ack Annie was a B-17G, serial 42-32095, that fought with the 95th Bomb Group.

Superstitious Al-O-Ysius was a B-17F, serial 42-37807, that served with the 100th Bomb Group.

A B-17F, serial 42-3442, *Hell's Chariot*, that fought with the 96th Bomb Group.

Old Crow served with the 303rd Bomb Group

Kipling's Error the III, was a B-17F, serial 42-5885, that fought with the 338th Bomb Squadron, 96th Bomb Group.

Hells-Belles, was a B-17G that fought with the 388th Bomb Group.

Esky was a B-17G, serial 42-31946, that fought with the 333rd Bomb Squadron, 94th Bomb Group. Esky was the mascot for *Esquire* magazine.

Nine Little Yanks and a Jerk was a B-17F, serial 42-3271, that fought with the 100th Bomb Group.

Cash & Carrie, a B-17F, serial 42-31134, was assigned to the 569th Bomb Squadron, 390th Bomb Group.

Our Buddy, a B-17G, that fought with the 452nd Bomb Group. This aircraft was named in honor of the P-47 fighters that escorted the bombers during missions.

The mission markings on this B-17 show bull's eyes on all four targets.

Black Hawk, a B-17F, that fought with the 96th Bomb Group.

Heaven Can Wait.

The B-17G *Boobie Trap* fought with the 351st Bomb Group.

Little Boy Blue, a B-17F, serial 42-30851, belonged to the 560th Bomb Squadron, 388th Bomb Group.

Pistol Packin Mama saw a lot of action as evidenced by the numerous mission marks.

This B-17G was dubbed *Queen of the Ball* by members of the 511th Bomb Squadron, 351st Bomb Group.

This crew took time to have a group photo taken in front of its B-17, *Rigor-Mortis.*

Ole Blood-N-Guts, a B-17G, serial 42-107078, belonged to the 603rd Bomb Squadron, 398th Bomb Group.

Plutocrate, a B-17F, serial 42-52455, was assigned to the 458th Bomb Group.

Look at the spots on this B-17, serial 42-441, used as a formation aircraft.

Cock O' The Walk, serial 42-30800, was assigned to the 388th Bomb Group. This aircraft was lost on 29 February 1944.

Smilin' Sandy Sanchez was a B-17G, serial 42-97290, assigned to the 334th Bomb Squadron, 95th Bomb Group.

This 385th Bomb Group B-17, serial 42-3544, was named *Stars and Stripes*.

The famous words, "We the People," found their way onto the nose of this B-17F, serial 41-24614, that served with the 422nd Bomb Squadron, 305th Bomb Group.

This B-17G, *Shoo Shoo Shoo Baby,* serial 42-32076, was interned in Sweden for the duration of the war. Upon her return to the United States, *Shoo* was restored by the Air Force Reservists at Dover AFB, Delaware.

This B-17G, *Texas Raiders,* is based in Houston. A representative of the Confederate Air Force, she proudly displays her new motif and paint scheme at the Aerospace America Air Show in Oklahoma City, June 1991.

The B-17G *Sentimental Journey* is another representative of the Confederate Air Force and is home-based with the Arizona Wing.

General Ike, a B-17G, serial 42-97061, fought with the 91st Bomb Group. The art was painted by Tony Starcer. Eisenhower christened the aircraft in April 1944.

Tom Paine, a B-17F, serial 42-30793, that served with the 388th Bomb Group, carries the quote, "Tyranny, like hell, is not easily conquered."

Sally B, a B-17G belonging to and sponsored by S.A.S., is seen on the hard stand in England as part of the historical preservation efforts in the United Kingdom.

Memphis Belle, a B-17F, serial 41-24485, assigned to the 91st Bomb Group, 8th Air Force was the first B-17 to see 25 combat missions over Europe. Plane and crew returned to the United States for War Bond drives.

Miss Barbara, serial 41-24519, was a B-17F that served with the 8th Air Force.

Fifinella was a Walt Disney character adopted by the Women's Air Service Pilots (WASPs).

Nine O Nine, a B-17G, serial 42-31909, served with the 91st Bomb Group.

Sweet and Lovely, a B-17F, serial 42-30721, was assigned to the 381st Bomb Group.

Balls of Fire, serial 42-109796, was assigned to the 445th Bomb Group.

The art on *Mother and Country,* serial 42-5703, was designed for the movie *Memphis Belle.* Numerous B-17s were reunited for this epic film.

This B-17F, *Baby Ruth,* serial 41-24335, was another of the B-17s used in *Memphis Belle.*

Aluminum Overcast, a B-17G, was converted to civil duty after the war and lost its chin turret in the transition.

Wicked Wanda is on static display.

Picadilly Lilly II, serial 483684, was used in the TV series, *12 O'Clock High,* and in the movie of the same name.

C-Cup, another creation for *Memphis Belle,* carries the same serial, 41-24335, as that of the B-17 *Baby Ruth.*

Short Bier, a B-17G-90-DL, serial 44-83663, is one of the surviving Fortresses on static display.

Miss Liberty Belle, a B-17G-90-DL, serial 44-83690, is another example of a fine restoration.

King Bee, serial 42-3474, was a veteran of the bloody 100th Bomb Group and is on static display.

Mary Alice, a B-17G that served with the 401st Bomb Group, is shown on Display at the RAF museum at Duxford.

I'll Be Around is a B-17 in storage at Lackland Air Force Base, Texas.

Miss Carry was B-17F 42-30325, assigned to the 390th Bomb Group. Note the word "censored."

The B-17G *L'il Eight Ball.*

Cock O' The Sky was a B-17G that served with the 447th Bomb Group.

The B-17F *Red Gremlin*.

Calamity Jane was used as a training aircraft in the states after its last mission. This photo was taken at Amarillo Army Air Field.

The *Klap-Trap II*, serial 42-30130, was assigned to the 96th Bomb Group in Snetterton Heath, England.

Hulcher's Vultures, serial 42-39845, fought with the 388th Bomb Group.

The *Passionate Witch*, a B-17F, was assigned to the 385th Bomb Group.

Gung Ho, serial 42-31134, was assigned to the 569th Bomb Squadron, 390th Bomb Group. It crashed at Nurnburg on 9 October 1944.

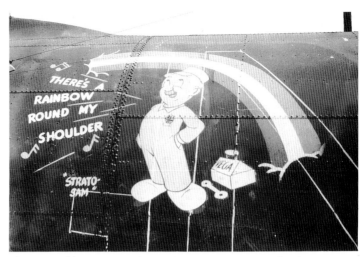

Elmer Fudd is pictured on *Strato-Sam,* a Vega-built B-17 assigned to the 303rd Bomb Group. It carried the song title, "There's A Rainbow Round My Shoulder."

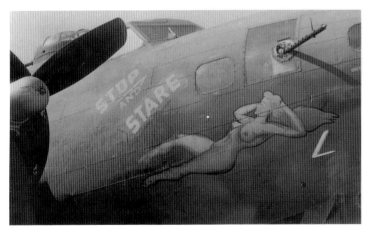

Stop And Stare. As one can imagine, that happened quite often.

Elmer Fudd wears a bunny suit, and announces, "We Have Some Extra Special Eggs for the Axis This Easter!" This work is also signed *Strato-Sam.*

The 92nd Bomb Group B-17F *Exterminator* pictured Hitler's head caught in the small portion of a V.

Duchess' Daughter, a B-17G, serial 42-97272, joined the 303rd Bomb Group on 19 April 1944. At the time of this photo she had been on only four missions.

Sky Chief, a B-17G, was assigned to the 385th Bomb Group.

"S" For Sugar, a B-17E, serial 41-24619, was piloted by 2nd Lt. Thomas L. Simmons of the 427th Bomb Squadron, 303rd Bomb Group. This aircraft was lost 11 January 1944 when it crashed near Braunlage.

The B-17 *Shackeroo.*

Holy Terror III, a B-17G, serial 42-40062, was assigned to the 100th Bomb Group.

Bugs Bunny munches a carrot on this B-17, *Round Twip Wabbit,* that served with the 379th Bomb Group.

Scarlett O'Hara, a B-17F, was assigned to the 379th Bomb Group.

This B-17, serial 42-3352, was named *Virgins Delight.* It was assigned to the 94th Bomb Group.

Wabbit-Twacks III, a B-17F, serial 42-30040, was assigned to the 96th Bomb Group. This art was by Sgt. Johnnie White.

This ill-fated B-17G named *Goering's Nightmare* was assigned to the 96th Bomb Group. The artwork is by Johnnie White.

Fertile Myrtle 3rd, serial 42-30366, was assigned to the 96th Bomb Group, 8th Air Force.

Stingy, a B-17G, serial 42-31053, was assigned to the 96th Bomb Group.

This B-17, *Windy City Avenger,* serial 42-3037, started its career with the 384th Bomb Group and later transferred to the 305th Bomb Group.

Virginia Lee II, a B-17G, fought with the 447th Bomb Group.

Hustlin' Hussy, a B-17F, serial 42-30354, was assigned to the 385th Bomb Group.

Sack Time, serial 42-5914, was assigned to the 385th Bomb Group, 8th Air Force. This photo was taken at Great Ashfield Airdrome in England.

Slo-Jo, serial 42-30168, was assigned to the 385th Bomb Group.

Hit Parade Jr, was a B-17G assigned to the 385th Bomb Group.

The B-17F *Big Red,* serial 42-30207, was assigned to the 561st Bomb Squadron, 388th Bomb Group.

The Floose, a B-17 that served with the 303rd Bomb Group, started her career in May 1944. Before the end of December the same year, she had piled up an amazing total of 100 missions without a mechanical abort.

This B-17E has not only been to the Pacific, as the sign says, but it returned to serve as a trainer at Amarillo Army Air Field.

San Antonio Rose, a B-17E, also saw combat in the Pacific, as noted by the scoreboard. It returned to Amarillo Army Air Field, to be used for pilot training.

Yankee Girl, a B-17G, serial 42-29557, served with the 305th Bomb Group and the 384th Bomb Group.

This B-17F, *Old Reliable,* returned from England to Amarillo Army Air Field, to serve as a trainer.

The B-17F *Doodle* shows off its heritage with the Hell's Angels by the scoreboard on its nose. This photo was taken at Amarillo Army Air Field.

Bundles for Berlin was assigned to the 92nd Bomb Group.

Black Diamond Express, a B-17F, also returned to the states to Amarillo Army Air Field.

The B-17F *Zoot Boys Pride.*

The crew poses in front of this 92nd Bomb Group B-17, *Carol Jane*, serial 42-97121.

Gremlin Castle, a B-17F, serial 42-29850, flew with the 351st Bomb Group. This aircraft was also among those at Amarillo Army Air Field.

The camera caught the crew pulling maintenance on the top turret of *Sugar Puss*, a B-17F piloted by Lt. Clarence Christman of the 544th Bomb Squadron, 384th Bomb Group.

The B-17F *Royal Flush*.

Homesick Angel, a B-17G, serial 42-31591, started its service with the 401st Bomb Group and later transferred to the 457th.

The B-17G *Lucky Partners* was assigned to the 447th Bomb Group, 8th Air Force.

Target For Tonite, a B-17F, carries an impressive scoreboard that shows seventy-five bomb missions during which the crew shot down fourteen Luftwaffe aircraft. This shot was taken at Amarillo Army Air Field.

The B-17F *Sweet Sue (Alias Bo-Peep)*.

This photo was taken after a crash landing by the B-17G *Rack and Ruin*. This aircraft was assigned to the 835th Bomb Squadron, 486th Bomb Group.

"I Came Here To Talk For Joe!" was the message on this B-17.

Picklepuss, a B-17F, serial 42-30063, was assigned to the 418th Bomb Squadron, 100th Bomb Group.

The Vibrant Virgin, a B-17F, serial 42-30275, was assigned to the 548th Bomb Squadron, 385th Bomb Group.

The B-17G *Big Stupe* has a unique mission scoreboard inside a big V for Victory. This aircraft belonged to the 545th Bomb Squadron, 384th Bomb Group.

This crew named its B-17F *Mugwump*.

Merrie Hell, a B-17F, serial 42-30046, that fought with the 546th Bomb Squadron, 384th Bomb Group.

Another bomb mission mark is going on this B-17F that served with the Hell's Angels, the 303rd Bomb Group.

The devil with his pitchfork aimed downward sends a definite message to the viewer of this B-17, *Hellzapoppin,* assigned to the 92nd Bomb Group.

This B-17F *Old Patch*, serial 43-38132, served with the 849th Bomb Squadron, 490th Bomb Group. This photo was taken at Amarillo Army Air Field.

Lady Satan, a B-17G, serial 42-97175, that fought with the 728th Bomb Squadron, 452nd Bomb Group.

The B-17G *Star Dust* fought with the 385th Bomb Group. This photo was taken at Great Ashfield.

The B-17G *Maggie's Drawers*.

The camera caught this name going on the B-17G *5 Grand*. This aircraft flew with the 96th Bomb Group and carried the serial 43-37716.

The B-17G *Hi-Blower* served with the 452nd Bomb Group. This photo was taken at the Kingman boneyard.

The B-17 *Esky* from the 385th Bomb Group. *Esky* was the mascot of *Esquire* magazine.

The B-17F *The Duchess.*

Jimmie Boy II was a B-17F that fought with the 94th Bomb Group. Note the name on the front hatch: "Chuck's Chop House."

The B-17F *My Devotion.*

Here's an example of how the art goes on. This B-17, 42-30378, named *Good Time Cholly III,* fought with the 331st Bomb Squadron, 94th Bomb Group.

High Life, a B-17F, serial 42-30080, fought with the 351st Bomb Squadron, 100th Bomb Group.

Our Bridget, a B-17F, is pictured being christened by its namesake.

This shot shows the serious damage inflicted on the B-17F *King Bee.,* serial 42-3474, that served with the 351st Bomb Squadron, 100th Bomb Group.

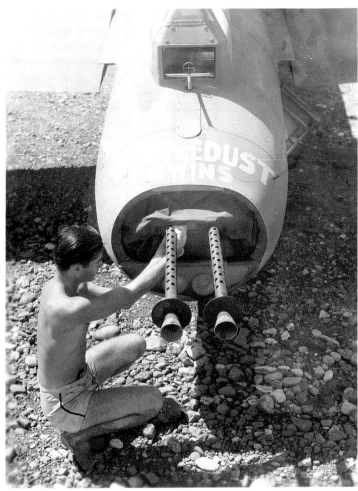

Each member of a B-17's crew often painted their own art. This tailgunner named his weapons *The Woofledust Twins.*

Ooold Soljer, serial 41-24559, was the flagship for the 360th Bomb Squadron.

Smashing Time!, a B-17G, serial 43-38158, fought with the 534th Bomb Squadron, 381st Bomb Group.

The B-17G *Anxious Angel.*

The B-17G *Feather Merchant*, serial 43-37644, that fought with the 728th Bomb Squadron, 452nd Bomb Group.

Ole Miss Destry was a B-17G, serial 42-31501, that served with the 366th Bomb Squadron, 305th Bomb Group.

Screamin' Eagle, a B-17G, serial 44-8007, fought with the 545th Bomb Squadron, 384th Bomb Group.

Hitler's Headache, a B-17G, serial 43-39180, that fought with the 600th Bomb Squadron, 398th Bomb Group. This photo was taken at Bradley Field, Connecticut.

The B-17G *Lucky Strike.*

The insignia of the 93rd Bomb Squadron found its way onto B-17E *Suzy-Q.* The 93rd served with the 19th Bomb Group.

The B-17G *Old Glory.*

The B-17F *I Got Spurs.*

This airborne B-17F, serial 42-29475, carried the skull and cross-bones and was named *Stric Nine*. It flew with the 323rd Bomb Squadron, 91st Bomb Group.

Songoon, a B-17G, serial 43-37563, is pictured at Bradley Field, Connecticut.

Miss Prudy, serial 44-8556, fought with the 34th Bomb Group. Note the name and art on the chin turret.

The B-17G *Purty Chili* fought with the 34th Bomb Group. The name referred to the weather in England, where the group was stationed.

Little Gismo, serial 44-6938, fought with the 34th Bomb Group.

Whizzer was a B-17F assigned to the 301st Bomb Group, serial 42-5419.

The B-17F *Cabin Heater*.

The art on *Whizzer* was also applied to the vertical.

Just Plain Lonesome, serial 42-39975, fought with the 324th Bomb Squadron, 91st Bomb Group.

The B-17G *D-Day Doll* is sitting in the boneyard after the war, as happened to most of the surviving aircraft. While she was active, she served with the 447th Bomb Group stationed at Rattlesden, England, from 29 November 1943 to 1 August 1945.

The B-17F *Slick Chick* fought with the 301st Bomb Group.

B-17G 42-29557, *Yankee Gal,* served with the 305th Bomb Group and the 84th Bomb Group.

The Wolf, a B-17F, fought with the 301st Bomb Group.

This B-17F was named for the super hero, *The Green Hornet*.

The B-17G *Sheriff's Posse*, serial 42-97151, fought with the 323rd Bomb Squadron, 91st Bomb Group.

Mary Cary, serial 42-97405, fought with the 360th Bomb Squadron, 303rd Bomb Group.

The B-17G *Sweet Melody*.

Wa-Hoo!, a B-17F, serial 41-24468, fought with the 369th Bomb Squadron, 306th Bomb Group.

A runaway propeller ate into the side of *Bonnie-B.*

Cindy, a B-17F, serial 42-5821 fought with the 527th Bomb Squadron, 379th Bomb Group.

The Sweater Girl fought with the 379th Bomb Group.

The Biggest Bird, a B-17G, serial 43-38306, fought with the 322nd Bomb Squadron, 91st Bomb Group.

Man O War II Horsepower Ltd., a B-17G, serial 42-38083, fought with the 322nd Bomb Squadron, 91st Bomb Group.

Queenie, a B-17G, serial 42-31353, fought with the 322nd Bomb Squadron, 91st Bomb Group.

The Joker's Wild was a B-17F, serial 41-24531.

Golden Gate In 48, was a B-17G, serial 44-8482, that fought with the 34th Bomb Group.

The B-17F *Carol Jean IV.*

The Sad Sack was a B-17F, serial 41-24504, that belonged to the 324th Bomb Squadron, 91st Bomb Group.

The B-17F *Temptation.*

This top turret on a B-17 carried the name *Louise*.

The B-17G *Princess Pat*, serial 42-102453, served with the 358th Bomb Squadron, 303rd Bomb Group.

Missbehaven Raven, a B-17G, serial 43-38280, had painted on it a wounded bird saying, "No Flak! Huh?"

This art was on a B-17G that served with the 303rd Bomb Group.

The art on the B-17F *Desperate Journey* shows the noble American eagle flying with Hitler held tightly in its talons.

Boots IV, serial 42-37850, served with the 413th Bomb Squadron, 96th Bomb Group.

I Do Dit was a B-17F that served with the 91st Bomb Group.

Being admired is the B-17F *Spirit of the Union Pacific*.

Dragon Lady, serial 42-30836, fought with the 551st Bomb Squadron, 385th Bomb Group. This aircraft was reported missing in action in February 1944.

Black Hawk, serial 42-30180, fought with the 337th Bomb Squadron, 96th Bomb Group. Note the small girl art on the nose with the name *Bette Lore*.

Flyin' Ginny, serial 42-3552, fought with the 339th Bomb Squadron, 96th Bomb Group.

Gypsy Princess, belonged to the 385th Bomb Squadron.

Fightin' Pappy, serial 42-5407, served with the 91st Bomb Group, 306th Bomb Group, and the 379th Bomb Group. It was reported missing in action 9 October 1943.

The B-17G *Madam Shoo Shoo*.

The B-17G *Mis Behavin*.

This art is from the B-17G *Mutz*.

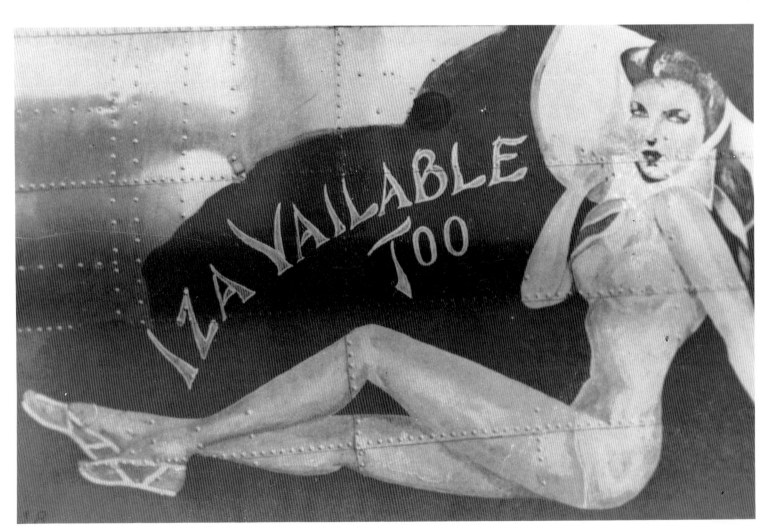

Iza Vailable Too, serial 42-97254, fought with the 360th Bomb Squadron, 303rd Bomb Group.

Sack Time, a B-17F, serial 42-5914, fought with the 549th
Bomb Squadron, 385th Bomb Group.

Mr. Lucky, a B-17G, serial 42-38035, belonged to the 385th
Bomb Group.

This art was saved from the B-17G *Nobby's Harriet Z.*

Rikki Tikki Tavi, a B-17F, serial 42-3324, fought with the 339th Bomb Squadron, 96th Bomb Group.

The B-17F *Spare Parts.*

Yankee Gal, a B-17F, serial 42-29557, served with the 365th
Bomb Squadron, 384th Bomb Group.

Daisy Mae was on the nose of the B-17G *Ragged But Right*, serial
42-97790, that served with the 385th Bomb Group.

This art was on the B-17G *Rum & Coke*, serial 44-8584.

The B-17F *Texas Raiders* belongs to the Houston Wing of the Confederate Air Force.

An unnamed B-17F.

The B-17G *Earthquake McGoon.*

The B-17F *Margie Mae,* serial 42-3847.

Stingy, a B-17G, serial 42-31053, fought with the 338th Bomb
Squadron, 96th Bomb Group.

The B-17F *Flak Hack*, serial 42-97329, served with the 360th
Bomb Squadron, 303rd Bomb Group.

Wabash Cannonball, a B-17F.

One of the most famous B-17s is the *Memphis Belle*, belonging
to the 324th Bomb Squadron, 91st Bomb Group.

Index